CPR

THE BIBLICAL GUIDE TO SOUL WINNING

CPR

THE BIBLICAL GUIDE TO SOUL WINNING

Aaron & Theresa McMahan

PO Box 464, Miamitown, Ohio 45041

Copyright, 2021

Aaron & Theresa McMahan

No part of this book may be reproduced either in printed form, electronically, or by any other means without the express written permission of the author. Said letter of permission must be displayed at the front of any electronically reproduced file.

ISBN 978-1-942050-23-0

Library of Congress Control Number: 2021911896

Preface

January 31, 2016 is a day I will never forget. It is the day when a young man witnessed to me on my best friend's front porch. I was an agnostic who had been searching for truth for some time. I had been raised in an agnostic household and we did not attend any type of religious services. It was left up to us to decide what we wanted to believe.

There were times through the years that I considered myself an atheist and other times where I became interested in new age practices including the occult. One of my great-grandmothers was involved in the occult and taught me a few things here and there.

At the ripe age of 29 I "had it made" in worldly standards. I "lived it up" every weekend, but years of that lifestyle weighed heavy on me. Alcohol and promiscuity no longer had the appeal they once held and they seemed to leave me hollow and longing for something I couldn't put my finger on.

In the summer of 2015, I felt an intense calling to hike the Appalachian Trail. A family friend had hiked it when I was younger and I remember hearing bits and pieces of the story. I felt that the 2,189 mile hike might be what could fix me and finally fill that void in my soul. I spent roughly 6 months preparing for the hike and in the process met other hikers through social media.

One of the hikers I met was Aaron McMahan. He was from Tennessee and I lived in Indiana. We chatted occasionally on social media but one day he offered to drive up and meet me. Our date went well, and I thought he was a very nice guy. I was glad to have met another hiker that would be out hiking during the same time frame.

Before he hopped in his little red truck to drive home, he witnessed to me. I had been to church a few times in my life with friends and I had heard of Jesus. There was even a guy who came to our school once and did a "chalk talk" while telling the story of Jesus' life. At the end he asked everyone to bow their heads and told us to raise our hand if we wanted to be saved and told us to "ask Jesus into our heart." I raised my hand, but I didn't really understand what any of it meant. All I knew was this Jesus guy sounded like the real deal.

Fast forward many years and there I was setting on my atheist best friend's porch as a guy I just met starts asking me which commandments I had broken. I was in the mindset that I had done more good in life than bad, so surely I would make it into Heaven. It didn't take long for me to realize that I had a big problem with sin and that I was on my way to hell. Aaron immediately told me the good news of the gospel and it was as if a light bulb had finally turned on in my soul. I finally understood what it meant to be saved and have eternal life.

As they say, the rest is history. Aaron and I hiked half of the Appalachian Trail together in 2016, got married in 2017, and adopted our daughter in 2019. Never underestimate the path that God has put you on, He has a plan for us all.

Table of Contents

Introduction 1
    The Great Commission 3
    The Importance of Prayer in Soul Winning 5

Soul Winning With CPR 7
    What is CPR? 7
    The Woman at the Well 9
    The Rich Young Ruler 15
    C: Creating Conversations 19
    P: Providing the Moral Law & the Good News
        Part 1 25
        The Good Person Test 27
        Part 2 33
    R: Repentance & Calling 37

False Gospels 41
Who, When, and Where 47
Common Mistakes 49
Checklist 51
Witness List 53

Introduction

The sun is setting on an average nothing new kind of day. A stroll through town is a sure way to clear your mind of anxieties and social dilemmas.

"Somebody, please help!" A panic-stricken bystander calls to you. An unconscious man is lying on the sidewalk not breathing. His lips and fingers are blue from the lack of oxygen.

Raw adrenaline courses through your veins. Your mind flashes to that CPR class to which you were invited, but never attended. Knowing you cannot help the man; you walk past his lifeless body.

This situation might sound terrible, but it is a similar to what most Christians face on a daily basis. Each day we walk past people who are dying spiritually and are in dire need of salvation through the life-giving gospel of grace.

To offer this life-saving gift to someone, you will need to know how. This guide will teach you how with a spiritual CPR technique. It will provide the tools that are necessary to reach out to the lost and dying souls that you come in contact with.

It is written in Scripture that those who win souls are wise (Proverbs 11:30). We should all be doing our part to save as many people as we can from an eternal, burning hell.

The Great Commission

We would like to commend you on taking the first step to becoming a soul winner. All Christians are called by our Lord Jesus Christ to the Great Commission, but sadly only few answer. We are told by the Lord Jesus in Matthew 9:37 that the "harvest truly is plenteous, but the labourers are few." When He spoke to the disciples after His resurrection, He told them to go and teach all nations (Matthew 28:19, Mark 16:15). The use of "all nations" refers to everyone on earth no matter their religious background or belief.

Many references are made in the Scriptures regarding *The Great Commission*. Listed below are a few verses that can help guide your study on what God has called us to do. While studying this guide, we urge you to highlight, mark, or add tabs to important verses in your Bible. Doing so will save you time during witness interactions. In this guide we will be using the 1611 King James Bible, as we believe it is the authorized version of God's inspired and preserved Word to us.

- ☐ Psalm 96:3
- ☐ 1 Chronicles 16:24
- ☐ Luke 10:1-24
- ☐ Acts 8:4
- ☐ Acts 13:47
- ☐ Romans 10:14-17
- ☐ 1 Corinthians 9:16
- ☐ 1 Corinthians 11:1
- ☐ 2 Corinthians 5:20
- ☐ 2 Timothy 4:5
- ☐ 1 Peter 3:15

The Importance of Prayer in Soul Winning

Prayer is vital in the life of every Christian. Through prayer, the Holy Spirit can provide you with the patience and wisdom needed to share the gospel, or good news, of our Lord Jesus Christ. Some people will not react kindly to the gospel message; thus, it is important that you exercise patience and loving-kindness during these encounters. The Apostle Paul stated preaching of the cross is foolish to those that are perishing (1 Corinthians 1:18), and knowing this before you share the gospel will help you understand how they may possibly react.

There are two main reasons why some Christians do not share the gospel; the first is **Lack of Knowledge** and the second is **Fear**. This knowledge can be gained by learning our CPR technique for soul winning. Overcoming fear may be difficult, but God does not give us the spirit fear (2 Timothy 1:7-8). Satan will do his best to instill fear in you so that you do not share the gospel. Pray without ceasing and put on the full armor of God (Ephesians 6:10-20). We are equipped with the Word of God and Satan is no match for that two-edged sword (Hebrews 4:12).

We also cannot forget to pray for the lost person with whom we share the gospel. While we may be planting and watering in God's garden, He is always the one who gives the increase (1 Corinthians 3:6-7). Ask in faith and trust that God will provide exactly what that person needs at that time to receive the Lord Jesus Christ (James 1:6).

Soul Winning With CPR

What is CPR?

CPR is an emergency medical procedure used to aid someone who is not breathing. CPR can be life-saving, but only if the proper methods are used. This Christian version of CPR can also be life-saving by presenting the gospel correctly. Most churches in modern Christianity simply do not know how to properly present the gospel. When presented correctly, the gospel of our Lord can save a person's soul from eternal damnation in Hell if they choose to accept it.

When you learn this technique, you will begin to notice how many people around you need this life-saving gift. There are three basic components to our version of CPR.

C - Creating Conversations.
P - Providing the Moral Law and the Good News
R - Repentance and Calling

It is necessary that we follow the Lord Jesus Christ's method when presenting the good news of the gospel to unbelievers. For example, the Lord Jesus Christ brought his message with loving-kindness; He did not argue and He never lost His disposition, not even when He was pushed by those who mocked and ridiculed Him. His interactions only consisted of presenting the moral law to the prideful and the gospel of grace to the humble.

The next few pages take a look at how the Lord Jesus Christ spoke with the woman at the well (John 4:1-30) and the rich young ruler (Matthew 19:16-30, Mark 10:17-31, Luke 18:18-30). We will be breaking down the key points of these conversations. This will help you understand why we use the CPR method.

It is important to remember that you are not the one doing the saving. All you will do is present the moral law and the gospel. It is for each person to use their free-will to either accept or reject the gospel.

The Woman at the Well
John 4:6-29

Scripture (KJV)	CPR
	C: Creating Conversations
⁶Now Jacob's well was there. Jesus therefore, being wearied with his journey, sat thus on the well: and it was about the sixth hour.	
⁷There cometh a woman of Samaria to draw water: Jesus saith unto her, Give me to drink.	Natural Conversation
⁹Then saith the woman of Samaria unto him, How is it that thou, being a Jew, askest drink of me, which am a woman of Samaria? for the Jews have no dealings with the Samaritans.	
¹⁰Jesus answered and said unto her, If thou knewest the gift of God, and who it is that saith to thee, Give me to drink; thou wouldest have asked of him, and he would have given thee living water.	Conversation Transition

¹¹ The woman saith unto him, Sir, thou hast nothing to draw with, and the well is deep: from whence then hast thou that living water?

¹² Art thou greater than our father Jacob, which gave us the well, and drank thereof himself, and his children, and his cattle?

¹³ Jesus answered and said unto her, Whosoever drinketh of this water shall thirst again:

¹⁴ But whosoever drinketh of the water that I shall give him shall never thirst; but the water that I shall give him shall be in him a well of water springing up into everlasting life.

Spiritual Conversation

Scripture (KJV)

CPR

P: Providing the Moral Law & the Good News

¹⁵ The woman saith unto him, Sir, give me this water, that I thirst not, neither come hither to draw.

¹⁶ Jesus saith unto her, Go, call thy husband, and come hither.

¹⁷ The woman answered and said, I have no husband. Jesus said unto her, Thou hast well said, I have no husband:

Jesus used conviction of sin.

We use the moral law to provide conviction from the Holy Spirit.

¹⁸ For thou hast had five husbands; and he whom thou now hast is not thy husband: in that saidst thou truly.

¹⁹ The woman saith unto him, Sir, I perceive that thou art a prophet.

²⁰ Our fathers worshipped in this mountain; and ye say, that in Jerusalem is the place where men ought to worship.

²¹ Jesus saith unto her, Woman, believe me, the hour cometh, when ye shall neither in this mountain, nor yet at Jerusalem, worship the Father.

Jesus proclaims the gospel of his arrival as Messiah.

²² Ye worship ye know not what: we know what we worship: for salvation is of the Jews.

²³ But the hour cometh, and now is, when the true worshippers shall worship the Father in spirit and in truth: for the Father seeketh such to worship him.

²⁴ God is a Spirit: and they that worship him must worship him in spirit and in truth.

²⁵ The woman saith unto him, I know that Messias cometh, which is called Christ: when he is come, he will tell us all things.

²⁶ Jesus saith unto her, I that speak unto thee am he.

Note: Before the death, burial, and resurrection of Jesus, the gospel message was to believe on Him as the Messiah. We are now under the gospel of grace by faith in the finished work at the cross, as given to us by the Apostle Paul.

Scripture (KJV)	CPR
²⁷ And upon this came his disciples, and marvelled that he talked with the woman: yet no man said, What seekest thou? or, Why talkest thou with her? ²⁸ The woman then left her waterpot, and went her way into the city, and saith to the men, ²⁹ Come, see a man, which told me all things that ever I did: is not this the Christ?	**R: Repentance & Calling** The woman repented and believed. Calling was not needed because she was with Him in the flesh. She confessed to others that the Messiah has come.

The Rich Young Ruler
Matthew 19:16-26

Scripture (KJV)	CPR
	C: Creating Conversations
ⁱ⁶ And, behold, one came and said unto him, Good Master, what good thing shall I do, that I may have eternal life?	Natural Conversation
ⁱ⁷ And he said unto him, Why callest thou me good? there is none good but one, that is, God: but if thou wilt enter into life, keep the commandments.	Spiritual Conversation
	Note: The young man wants to know which works he can do to gain eternal life. Works are a natural conversation. Jesus transitions to the spiritual by bringing God's holiness into the conversation.

Scripture (KJV)	CPR
	P: Providing the Moral Law & the Good News
¹⁸ He saith unto him, Which? Jesus said, Thou shalt do no murder, Thou shalt not commit adultery, Thou shalt not steal, Thou shalt not bear false witness,	Moral Law is used to bring conviction and humility.
¹⁹ Honour thy father and thy mother: and, Thou shalt love thy neighbour as thyself.	
²⁰ The young man saith unto him, All these things have I kept from my youth up: what lack I yet?	The young man is self-righteous and not humble.
²¹ Jesus said unto him, If thou wilt be perfect, go and sell that thou hast, and give to the poor, and thou shalt have treasure in heaven: and come and follow me.	Jesus convicts the man's heart by saying he must deny his works and wealth. The man must trust alone in Jesus.

Scripture (KJV)	CPR
	R: Repentance & Calling
²² But when the young man heard that saying, he went away sorrowful: for he had great possessions.	The young man rejected the gospel.
²³ Then said Jesus unto his disciples, Verily I say unto you, That a rich man shall hardly enter into the kingdom of heaven.	
²⁴ And again I say unto you, It is easier for a camel to go through the eye of a needle, than for a rich man to enter into the kingdom of God.	Jesus teaches that relying on anything, including wealth, can keep a person from repentance.
²⁵ When his disciples heard it, they were exceedingly amazed, saying, Who then can be saved?	
²⁶ But Jesus beheld them, and said unto them, With men this is impossible; but with God all things are possible.	

C
Creating Conversations

The Lord Jesus Christ started out His interaction with the woman at the well in the natural world with a natural conversation by asking for a drink of water. Then He cleverly shifted the conversation from physical water to spiritual water. This shift from the natural to the spiritual can be nerve-racking for new soul winners. Even mature and experienced soul winners often get nervous before striking up a spiritual conversation. This is why we emphasize prayer to anyone that is learning to witness.

The Primary Challenge in Witnessing and How to Overcome It

You may meet someone like the rich young ruler who may try to bring a works-based spiritual conversation to you. The Church of Jesus Christ of Latter-day Saints (Mormon) and Jehovah's Witnesses, both of which are works-based religions, may come to your home and want to speak to you about their religious beliefs. Even though they are interested in speaking about spiritual topics, they still need to be witnessed to in the same way. The rich young man was stuck in his physical works for salvation, as are many people. The Bible calls these people heretics because they misquote the Scripture and lead people away from the Truth.

What You Should Do

Do not spend all of your time and effort trying to convert someone from a works-based religion. We are told that we should tell them the gospel not more than twice because they have decided to condemn themselves (Titus 3:10-11). For biblical references on dealing with works-based salvation and heretics, refer to the False Gospels chapter of this guide.

We have provided a few conversation starters in this section that should be able to help you begin a natural conversation and then transition into the spiritual. The spiritual realm is where the Holy Spirit dwells and exposing a person to the spiritual realm is crucial in this process. It allows God's word to soften and convict the conscience, which is required before they can understand repentance.

☐ Start a Natural Conversation

- Do you attend a church? Were you raised in a religious household? What do you think our purpose is for being here?
    - Make sure to truly listen and hear what a person has to say.
    - Politely keep the conversation on the topic that you started.
- What are some natural conversation starters you feel comfortable using? These will likely change throughout your life as you become involved in different hobbies, attend educational institutions, start a career, or as you start a family.

Natural Conversation Starters I Can Use:

1. _____
2. _____
3. _____
4. _____
5. _____

☐ Transition to a Spiritual Conversation

- What do you think happens when we die? Do you believe in an afterlife?
    - The answer you receive will give you the general worldview of what that person believes.

☐ If They Do Not Believe in an Afterlife

- Why do you believe there is no afterlife?
    - Do not get upset if they say they are an atheist or agnostic.
    - Push the conversation towards a hypothetical afterlife.
    - You can use apologetics sparingly, but avoid becoming trapped in natural conversations of science and philosophy. You want to bring them to the moral law, in which the conscience agrees, as quickly as possible.

Note: Many witnessing interactions come to this point and do not progress forward due to a lack to empathy on the part of the Christian and a lack of knowledge of worldviews. Your goal is not to force your belief on the person. You should show them respect and kindness and allow their conscience to reason through the questions you provide.

- Do you believe the scientific impossibility that "nothing created everything"?
    - Denying the afterlife because they do not believe in a creator:
        1. Use any item: phone, car, book, building, cup, etc. Did this item create itself or appear out of thin air? Did matter suddenly turn into that item?
        2. If the item has been created then someone must have created it. Not knowing the item's creator does not negate the fact that is was created.
        3. If the item cannot create itself. How can the universe create itself? How can DNA create itself before DNA existed? Chemical evolution (the creation of the elements) cannot evolve into biological evolution (creation of DNA and lifeforms). The belief of macro evolution requires more faith than a belief in a creator.
        4. If there is a creator, they must be an all-knowing and powerful being. Such a being would provide us with information about themselves and we believe that information is the Bible.

☐ The Afterlife: Are You Going to Heaven or Hell?

- Do you think you will go to a good place or bad place when you die?
- Do you think you are good enough to go to Heaven?
  - YES - Would you like to take a test to be certain?
  - NO - If they know they are a humble sinner that knows they are lost, skip the moral law test and go straight to the good news of the gospel.

Note: You may run into people who claim that the Bible teaches there is no such place as Hell or that it is not a place of torment and punishment. It is important that you understand what the Bible actually has to say about this. The Lord Jesus Christ spoke about Hell more than any other person in the Bible. Below are a few verses you can reference for Hell:

- Deuteronomy 32:22
- Proverbs 27:20
- Ezekiel 31:17
- Matthew 23:15, 33
- Luke 12:5
- 2 Peter 2:4
- Psalms 139:8
- Isaiah 5:14
- Matthew 5:22, 29-30
- Matthew 25:41
- Mark 9:43, 45, 47
- Luke 16:23-24

P
Providing the Moral Law & the Good News

Part 1

Our "Good Person Test" is based on the Bible's Ten Commandments. They are used to see if someone has been able to live up to God's standard of perfection. A person must be sinless to enter Heaven (John 3:3). Everyone has sinned and fallen short of God's standard (Romans 3:23). When a person is old enough to understand the difference between right and wrong God will hold them accountable for their thoughts and actions. We will be using the commandments as a mirror so a person can see their sinful nature. The law will be their judge, not us. The moral law of God is the perfect tool for providing conviction and bringing someone to repentance (Psalm 19:7). We are not calling them a sinner, instead we are letting them come to that conclusion on their own.

The Purpose of the Law in Soul Winning:

- o We say we are good, but the law shows otherwise (Proverbs 20:6).
- o The law provides the knowledge of sin and finds the whole world guilty (Romans 3:19-20).
- o Even the Apostle Paul, who was persecuting Christians, thought he was good until he came to the knowledge of his sin (Romans 7:7-9).
- o The law provides us a mirror to show us how sinful we are compared to God's perfection (James 1:23-25).
- o The law is good, just, holy, and spiritual (Romans 7:12-14).
- o The law shows us to be unclean and unrighteous in God's standard (Isaiah 64:6).

The Good Person Test
The Ten Commandments

- <u>Lying</u>: **Thou shalt not bear false witness against thy neighbor (Exodus 20:16).**
    - Have you ever told a lie or "white lie"?

- <u>Theft</u>: **Thou shalt not steal (Exodus 20:15).**
    - Have you ever stolen anything no matter the value of the item (piece of candy, illegally downloading music)?

- <u>Dishonoring Parents</u>: **Honor thy father and thy mother (Exodus 20:12).**
    - Did you ever disobey your parents? If you have broken any of the commandments it dishonors their name.

- <u>Blasphemy</u>: **Thou shalt not take the name of the Lord thy God in vain; for the Lord will not hold him guiltless (Exodus 20:7).**
    - Have you ever used God's name or title with dishonor?

- **Adultery**: Thou shalt not commit adultery (Exodus 20:14; Matthew 5:27-28).
  - Have you ever committed adultery? Have you ever looked at someone with lust?

- **Murder**: Thou shalt not kill (Exodus 20:13; Matthew 5:21-22).
  - Have you ever murdered someone? Have you ever hated someone or been angry without righteous cause (road rage, anger towards a family member)?

- **Coveting**: Thou shalt not covet (Exodus 20:17).
  - Have you ever desired something that belonged to someone else (house, car, career, wealth, physical appearance)?

- **Idolatry**: Thou shalt have no other gods before me (Exodus 20:3-4).
  - Have you always put God first in your life? Has anything ever been more important to you than God?

- **Sabbath**: Remember the Sabbath day, to keep it holy (Exodus 20:8).

Generally, you will not need to use all ten of the commandments. We recommend using 4-5 in most circumstances. Lying and stealing are good to start with. Adultery and murder are best kept until the end so you can include that our impure thoughts are also sins. If someone believes they are not "that bad" remind them that one offense of the law makes them guilty of all (James 2:10). Take a look at the next page where we use the commandments in an example.

Me: Have you ever told a lie?

Person: Yes, hasn't everyone?

Me: I know I have. What do you call someone who tells lies?

Person: A liar?

Me: Yep. Have you ever stolen anything, no matter the value?

Person: Well...maybe once when I was a kid.

Me: What do you call someone who steals things?

Person: A thief?

Me: Yep. Have you ever committed adultery?

Person: Oh no, I would never do that.

Me: The Bible says if we even look on someone with lust that we have committed adultery in our heart (Matthew 5:27-28). It's not just physical acts, but also our thoughts and feelings that matter.

Person: Yeah, I've done that, but hasn't everyone?

Me: I'm not sure about everyone, but I have. Have you ever killed anyone?

Person: Absolutely not!

Me: The Bible tells us that if we hate someone or are angry with them without cause we murder them in our heart (Matthew 5:21-22).

Person: Well I suppose I've done that too.

Me: So, by your own admission, you are telling me that you are a liar, a thief, an adulterer and murderer at heart.

Person: Yeah, I guess I have done all of that.

Me: Do you think God would send you to Heaven or Hell? Would He reward you for all the laws you broke?

- [ ] **When they admit they are a sinner ask them where they think they will go, Heaven or Hell?**
    - The unrighteous shall not inherit the kingdom of God. No fornicators, idolaters, or thieves shall inherit the kingdom of God (1 Corinthians 6:9-10).
    - There are none good, only God (Matthew 19:17).
    - All have sinned and come short of the glory of God. There is none that doeth good, no, not one (Romans 3:10-12, 23).

- [ ] **If they know they are sinner, but are relying on asking for forgiveness to get them into heaven.**
    - If you commit a crime can you ask the judge for forgiveness? Will they let you go without a fine? You still have to pay the fine or do the jail time as payment for breaking the law. Our crimes are against God and His fine is eternal (Hell).
    - God is the Judge of all people. Destruction will come to the workers of iniquity (Proverbs 21:15; Ecclesiastes 3:17; Hebrews 10:30; Romans 12:19).

- [ ] **If they think God will not send people to hell.**
    - If you receive the death penalty but refuse to believe in capital punishment does that change the outcome?
    - All liars, murderers, and idolaters will have their part in the lake of fire (Revelation 21:8).

P
Providing the Moral Law & the Good News

Part 2

- [ ] **The Gospel of Grace – The Free Gift of Salvation**
    - **Who is Jesus Christ?**
        - He is God in the flesh, the Son of God, and one part of the trinity of God (John 1:1-14, 3:16-17, 10:30; 1 John 3:22-23).
    - **What did Jesus Christ do?**
        - He lived a sinless life and fulfilled the law (1 Peter 2:22; Hebrews 4:15; 2 Corinthians 5:21).
        - He provided a blood atonement for our sin (Matt. 26:28; Colossians 1:20; Ephesians 1:7).
        - His blood was shed for the payment of our sins. He paid the fine for the laws we have broken (Acts 20:28; 1 Peter 2:24).
        - The Lord Jesus Christ was crucified, died, was buried, and was resurrected on the third day (1 Cor. 15:1-4; Matt. 28:5-6).
        - He conquered death (Revelation 1:18; Acts 2:24).

- Why Blood Atonement is Required
  - The life of the flesh is in the blood. Blood is required for an atonement for the soul (Leviticus 17:11, Hebrews 9:22).
  - Redemption is through Christ's blood and the forgiveness of sins is through the gift of grace (Ephesians 1:7; Romans 5:9).
- Who is the Apostle Paul?
  - He is the apostle to the gentiles. He provided us with the gospel of grace, which is salvation through faith alone in Christ's blood sacrifice. (Romans 11:13)

☐ **How to Explain the Gospel of Grace:**
- Once someone agrees they are a sinner, then you can present the gospel of grace to them.
- The person has lived under the moral law and has broken it, thereby they became unrighteous and unfit for Heaven. It is because of sin that we must die. God does not want the death of our souls (mind, will, and emotions) so He provided a solution.
- It is appointed for man once to die then to be judged (Hebrews 9:27). God has a day set aside where He will judge the world in righteousness (Acts 17:31). We will have to account for every sinful thought and action we did during our lives. God requires justice for the laws we have broken (Ecclesiastes 3:17).

- God entered into his creation as a man, to live under the law that we were subjected to and broke (Phil. 2:6-7). He kept a righteous account by never breaking the law (2 Cor. 5:21). Then He took upon himself in the flesh, the wrath of God for your sins (Romans 5:9). He was scourged, beaten, and hung on a cross to shed His sinless blood that was necessary for the remission of sins (John 19:1-42). He said "it is finished" and gave up the ghost (John 19:30; Luke 23:46).
- The Lord Jesus Christ was resurrected on the third day. He proved He was God incarnate by conquering death (John 20:8-9). The blood sacrifice He offered on our behalf was sufficient to pay our sin debt.
- After the resurrection, The Lord Jesus Christ walked the earth for 40 days (Acts 1:3). He was seen by more than 500 of His followers (1 Corinthians 15:6). After 40 days He ascended into Heaven and is sitting at the right hand of the Father (Acts 1:9).
- The Lord Jesus Christ offers us forgiveness for past, present, and future sins (Hebrews 9:26). Forgiveness of sin provides eternal life in Heaven when His righteousness is imputed to our account. This is a free gift that one must choose to receive.

R
Repentance & Calling

☐ **What is Repentance?**
- Turning away from one's self-righteousness (works-based religions, rituals, sacraments, unbelief, etc.) and toward the Lord Jesus Christ's righteousness. Trusting **alone** in the finished work at the cross (Luke 13:3; Matt. 9:13; Acts 17:30, 20:21).
- It is vitally important to understand that one does not turn from individual sins to be saved. One must turn from being a sinner to The Lord Jesus Christ. Individual sins are to be continually worked on after one is saved by support of the Holy Spirit (sanctification).

☐ **What Must One Believe?**
- To receive the gift of God's grace, one must agree with him that they are a sinner. They must believe in their heart that the Lord Jesus Christ was truly God and truly man. They have to believe He was crucified, died, and rose again to shed His blood to pay their personal sin debt (1 Cor. 15:1-4).
- God extends salvation by His grace, not of works (Ephesians 2:8-9). Grace is God's unmerited favor; that is received by faith.

- [ ] **Calling on God**
    - Believe in your heart and confess with your mouth to God that you are a sinner. All who call upon his name shall be saved (Romans 10:9-13; Revelation 3:20; Acts 2:21).
    - Even though salvation is personal between each person and God, it can be wise to offer a "template" for them on how to call on God for salvation.
        - "Lord, I come to you as a Sinner in need of a Savior. I realize if I die in my sins, that justice must be done and I will go to Hell. Your word says that even though I am a sinner, you love me enough to offer your son as a sacrifice on my behalf. His blood was shed to atone for my sins. I believe He was crucified, buried, and rose again. I am asking you to save me so I can go to Heaven. All this I ask in Jesus' name, Amen."

☐ What Next – Recommendations for a New Believer

- Read the Bible every day (KJV). We recommend starting with the Apostle Paul's books to understand more about the gospel of grace (Romans through Philemon).
- Find a church in your area that believes the Bible is the final authority.
- Pray every day. God speaks to you through His written word and we speak to Him through prayer.
- Submit to believers' baptism. Baptism does not save you, but it is a way to publicly profess your faith in Christ's death burial and resurrection.
- Give to God your time, talents, and treasure.
- Share your faith (Proverbs 11:30; Daniel 12:3).

False Gospels

A false gospel is a belief that anything other than faith in Jesus Christ is necessary for saving grace. Witnessing to people involved in false gospels can be exceptionally difficult. They do not know they are being deceived and may have hardened their heart to the gospel of grace. Paul, the Apostle to the gentiles (nations), said that if any person presents to you a gospel other than this, let them be accursed (Galatians 1:8). He warns us of those who will preach about "another Jesus" (2 Corinthians 11:4). He states that in the last days, people will depart from true faith and will follow doctrines of devils (1 Timothy 4:1).

Common False Gospels:
- Prosperity Gospel
- Lordship Salvation
- Suffer For Success or Poverty Gospel
- Salvation by Water Baptism
- New Age Spirituality Gospel
- God is Love and Not Judgement Gospel
- Signs and Wonders Gospel
- Social Justice Gospel
- God Knows My Heart Gospel
- Moralism Gospel
- Self Help Gospel

It is important for the soul winner to familiarize themselves with Acts 2:38. It is a favorite "go to" verse for many false "Christian" denominations who trust in water baptism for salvation. This includes immersion baptism or the "sprinkling" of babies. Those false teachings are relying on a works-based salvation with the baptism being the work. This is not the gospel given to the gentiles by the Apostle Paul.

Please note that most false gospels are a result of not obeying the Apostle Paul's teaching about "rightly dividing the word of truth" (2 Timothy 2:15). The entire Bible is given by the inspiration of God and is "for" us, but not all of it is directly "to" us. In Acts chapter 2, Peter was speaking to "the men of Judea" after the Messiah was crucified. The "men of Judea" asked, "What shall we do?" Peter responds in Acts 2:38, "Repent, and be baptized every one of you in the name of Jesus Christ for the remission of sins, and ye shall receive the gift of the Holy Ghost." The book of Acts transitioned doctrinally in chapter 8 when God called Paul to take the gospel of grace to the gentiles (nations).

It is imperative for the soul winner to understand the difference between the national Kingdom of Heaven doctrine and the Kingdom of God doctrine. The Kingdom of Heaven is a literal earthly reign of the Messiah in Jerusalem, as prophesied to Abraham in Genesis 12 and was offered in the Gospel's of Matthew, Mark, Luke, and John. The Kingdom of God doctrine introduced by Paul is righteousness, peace, and joy in the Holy Ghost. For further information on dividing the Bible we recommend studying Dispensationalism.

If you come across a belief system that originates from texts that oppose the Bible, you can still use the conscience to reach that person. Most religious belief systems use some form of the Ten Commandments. If you are witnessing to a person from a different religion (Muslim, Buddhist, Hindu, etc.) you can mention that their religion also has moral laws similar to the Bible's moral law.

Note: When witnessing to someone who believes in a false gospel, stand your ground. Do not get argumentative or angry and remember you are giving this message in loving-kindness. Always use Scripture to back up your beliefs.

Common Theological Disagreements and the Scripture that Supports the Truth:

- **The Bible is Full of Errors:**
    - 2 Timothy 3:16
    - Hebrews 1:1-2
    - 2 Peter 1:20-21

- **If God Exists Why is There Evil:**
    - Genesis 3:1-19
    - Isaiah 59:1-15
    - Romans 2:9, 3:9-20, 5:12-21

- **Denying the Trinity:**
    - Genesis 1:26
    - Matthew 28:18-20
    - 1 John 5:7

- **Denying Hell:**
    - Deuteronomy 32:22
    - Matthew 5:22, 18:9, 25:41
    - Luke 16:23-24

- **Denying Eternal Payment for Sin:**
    - Isaiah 66:22-23
    - Mark 9:44-48

- **Denying Christ is God (the deity of Christ):**
    - Isaiah 7:14, 9:6
    - John 1:1-14, 10:30
    - Zechariah 12:10
    - Matthew 1:23, 12:40, 18:20, 28:18-20
    - Mark 2:5-7, 11:2-6
    - Romans 3:23
    - 2 Corinthians 5:21
    - 1 Peter 3:18
    - 1 John 1:1, 5:7
    - Revelation 19:6

- **Man Can Become God or a god:**
    - Genesis 1:1
    - Malachi 3:6

- **Belief in False Prophets**
    - Isaiah 8:20

- **Believe Their Religion is the True Church**
    - Ephesians 4:4-6
    - Colossians 1:18-24

- **Relying on Works for Salvation**
    - John 15:6
    - Acts 4:12
    - Romans 4:5
    - Ephesians 2:8-9

- **Belief in Purgatory**
    - Psalm 49:6-9
    - Acts 8:20-23

- **What About People That Never Hear the Gospel**
    - Romans 1:18-21

Who, When, and Where

To Whom Should You Witness?

- Anyone!
- Your parents, grandparents, family members, friends, acquaintances, and even people you do not know.
- Make a witness list. Keep track of the people you plan on witnessing to so that you stay motivated.
- As you witness to each person on your list, keep track of who you have spoken to. This will help encourage you to keep pursuing those who you haven't spoken with.
- Make sure you pray before each witnessing encounter.

When Should You Witness?

- Anytime!
- There is no better time than now.
- Make sure you have enough time to have a thorough conversation before you start the interaction. Being rushed during this conversation is the last thing you want to worry about. Some conversations will go smoothly and may only take 10-15 minutes. Others may take 30-60 minutes if a person has many questions. This varies greatly depending on how much knowledge of the Bible someone has and what their world view is.

Where Should You Witness?

- Anywhere!
- There is no place that is off limits to God's power.
- Choose a place where you and the other person feel comfortable speaking about spiritual matters. This could be at home, in church, or in a public setting such as a coffee shop.
- For long distance friends and family, a simple telephone call works great. You can have your Bible in front of you and a checklist beside you to keep you on track during the conversation.
- Your church family is a great place to practice your skills. Born again Christians will welcome your enthusiasm to share the gospel.
- Once you have grown in confidence and ability, you can venture out to more public areas. Coffee shops, laundromats, and grocery stores are great places to strike up conversations.

Common Mistakes

- One on one conversations are best. As you gain confidence and wisdom you can approach groups of two or three people.

- Show love and genuine care for the person. One of the easiest ways to do this is to actively listen to what a person has to say.

- Do not react in anger or interrupt a person (Proverbs 15:1, Titus 3:2).

- Do not take rejection personally. Remember they have rejected Christ not you (Luke 10:16).

- Do not let them lead you down a rabbit hole. If you find the conversation trailing into another direction, politely bring it back around to the original conversation (2 Timothy 2:23-26).

CPR Checklist

Use this checklist to help guide you when first learning how to share the gospel. You can use this list to practice witnessing to born again Christians in your family or church. If you plan to witness to someone over the phone you can also keep this nearby to make sure you are staying on track with the conversation.

☐ C – CREATE A CONVERSATION

1. Start with a Natural Conversation
    Examples:
    How have you been?
    Are the kids doing well?
    How is your hobby going?

2. Transition to the Spiritual
    Examples:
    Do you attend a local church?
    Did you grow up in a religious household?
    Do you believe in an afterlife?

3. Continue Spiritual Conversation
    Are you a good person?
    Are you good enough to go to Heaven?

☐ P – PROVIDE THE MORAL LAW & THE GOOD NEWS

1. Have an idea of which commandments you want to use and write them down or mark them in your Bible.

2. Do not call someone a sinner, it is up to each person to admit they are a sinner.

3. Make sure you explain who Jesus was, what He did, and how His blood paid their fine for their sin.

☐ R – REPENTANCE & CALLING

1. Explain that repentance is turning to God and trusting alone in the finished work of The Lord Jesus Christ. Forsaking the idea that your good works will get you into Heaven. We are saved by grace alone, through faith alone, in Christ alone.

2. If one believes this, they can call on God in prayer or aloud to confess that they are a sinner and in need of God's free gift of salvation.

Witness List

Use this page to list out the friends, family, co-workers, and acquaintances that you would like to witness to. If they are Christians, you can still list them to practice using the CPR techniques. Check each name off after you witness to them.

☐ _____
☐ _____
☐ _____
☐ _____
☐ _____
☐ _____
☐ _____
☐ _____
☐ _____
☐ _____
☐ _____
☐ _____
☐ _____
☐ _____

Notes: